Contents

This book covers the following topics:

Unscramble these words using the Contents above to help you.

trompuce _____

yemmor _____

cropresso _____

ANSWERS: computer, memory, processor

Computers and data

Computers are electronic devices. They follow instructions to do useful things with **data**. Data is **information** like letters, numbers, photos and music.

Tick the boxes as you spot each computer device.

- ☐ robot
- ☐ tablet
- ☐ hand-held game
- ☐ webcam
- ☐ mobile phone
- ☐ laptop

The parts of a computer you can **touch** are called **hardware**. Apps (or applications) and data are called **software**.

Draw a circle around the **hardware**, and underline the **software**.

 digital music

 mouse

 photo editor

 website

 keyboard

 screen

 video player

 mobile phone

 game

 headphones

ANSWERS: Hardware = mouse, screen, keyboard, mobile phone, headphones; Software = digital music, photo editor, video player, game, website

Well done!

5

Inputs and outputs

A computer has **inputs** and **outputs** to get information in and out.

An **input device**, like a keyboard, mouse or game controller, sends information TO the computer.

From the list below, which do you think are **input devices**? Follow the lines to find out.

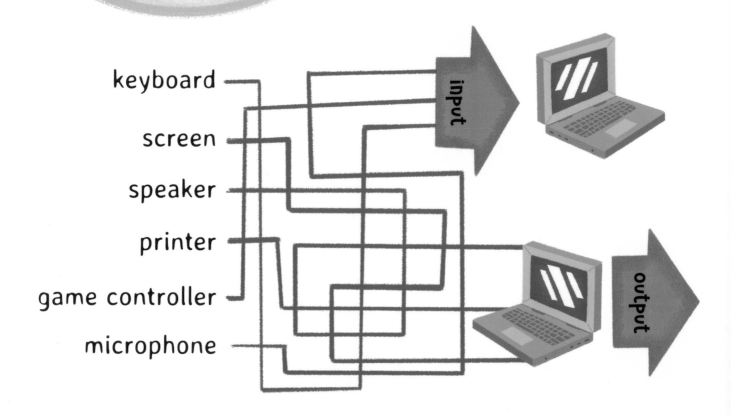

keyboard

screen

speaker

printer

game controller

microphone

input

output

ANSWERS: Input devices = keyboard, game controller, microphone; Output devices = screen, speaker, printer

An **output device** delivers information FROM the computer. Screens, speakers and printers are all **output devices**.

Tablets and phones have **inputs** and **outputs** in one device.

HI!

TOUCHSCREEN
acts as an input AND
output device

Use the words below to finish these sentences.

input

to

output

An _____ device delivers information from a computer.

A touchscreen acts as an output and _____ device.

An input device sends information _____ a computer.

Well done!

Circuit board

Under the screen of a **tablet**, it looks a bit like this:

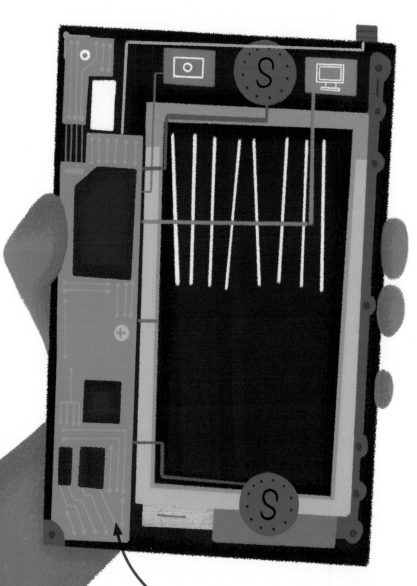

Circle these things when you spot them.

(S) speakers

[◦] camera

headphone jack

🖥 screen circuit board

battery

CIRCUIT BOARD connects all the parts together and relies on computer chips to do lots of jobs

COMPUTER CHIP is a slice of silicon with lots of electronics on it. This silicon is made from sand!

Computer chips and other parts of the computer are connected with **thin wires** printed onto the **circuit board**.

The **processor** is the most important computer chip. It **controls everything** and needs to be connected to all the other components.

Draw wires to connect the **processor** to all of the chips on the circuit board, without any **wires** crossing over.

Find out what these ICONS mean on p18

storage

memory

processor

motion sensor

Well done!

Processor and memory

The **processor** is like the **brain** of the computer. It can carry out many millions of **simple instructions** every second, but it can't remember much, so it uses **memory**.

How quickly can you draw lines to join up these numbers in the **right order?**

1

9

12

2

7

4

10

6

5

Wipe clean the activity and try to do it faster. You're using your **memory** to do this activity.

11

3

8

Memory is **faster** than storage. But when you turn a computer off, memory doesn't hold on to the information, only storage can do that.

Processor and memory

The **processor** reads **instructions** from memory. It reads and writes **data** so that it can complete (run) the instructions.

Can you be a **processor** and write in the correct answers?

INSTRUCTIONS

DATA

get a

add b

a+b=c

PROCESSOR

put c

get d

add e

d+e=f

put f

get g

add h

put i

memory

a = 4

b = 5

c = 9

d = 2

e = 6

f = ☐

g = ☐

h = ☐

i = ☐

memory

Fill in the missing parts to **process** the instructions. Can you make up your own?

Well done!

Storage

Most computers have **storage** to save entire **programs** and **data**. You can add more apps or data only if you have enough storage.

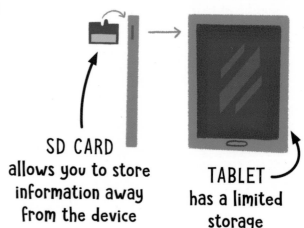

SD CARD allows you to store information away from the device

TABLET has a limited storage

Millie's tablet says there's not enough room to install a new app.

What could Millie ask a grown-up to do? Tick all the **correct** options to try.

☐ Delete some photos

☐ Tell the tablet to install the new app anyway

☐ Delete an app that isn't used any more

☐ Switch it off and on again

When you **delete** an app it often removes its data too, so always ask a grown-up first!

ANSWERS: Deleting some photos and an app that isn't used any more would work best

Computers need **electrical power** to work – some need to be plugged into a wall socket, some have a **rechargeable battery** inside them.

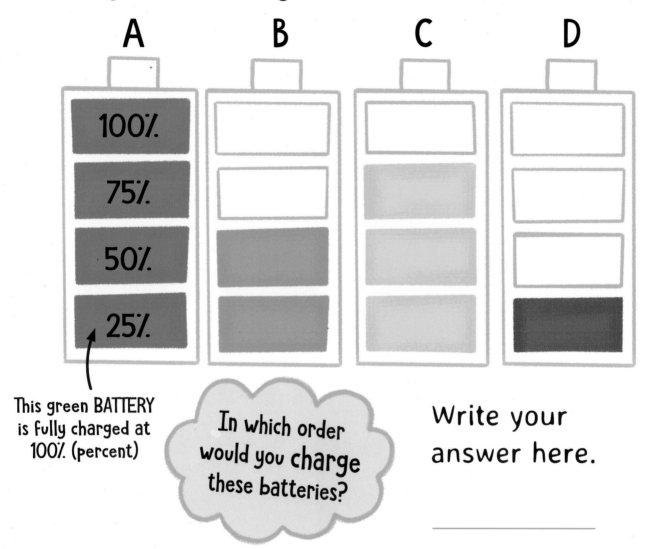

A   B   C   D

100%

75%

50%

25%

This green BATTERY is fully charged at 100% (percent)

In which order would you **charge** these batteries?

Write your answer here.

_____

Some **tiny computers** inside toys and gadgets use **batteries**, which you need to change when they run out.

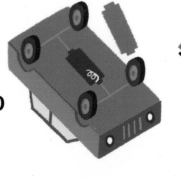

Well done!

Screens and pixels

A computer **screen** is made up of lots of tiny squares called **pixels**.

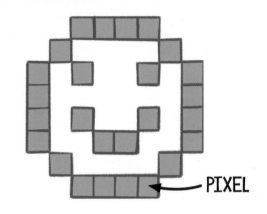
PIXEL

Can you copy the **pixel art** into this simple grid?

The **more pixels** a screen has, the better the picture.

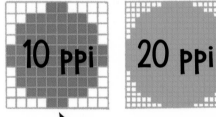

10 ppi 20 ppi 40 ppi

PPI means pixels per inch

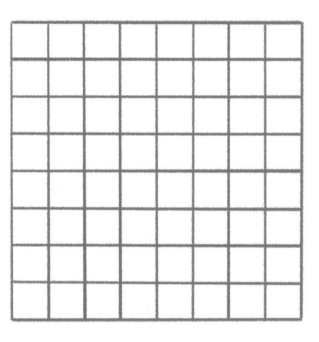

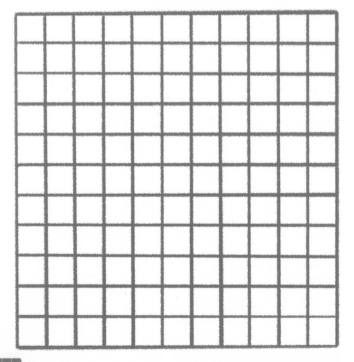

Now create your own pixel art in this grid.

Pixel colours are made by mixing together different amounts of **red**, **green** and **blue**.

How does a touchscreen work?

Touchscreens work because people conduct electricity (yes, YOU are conductive!).

A touchscreen has a **grid of wires** inside it, so it can work out where the change happened.

Touchscreens can spot a tap, swipe or pinch from you by the **electrical changes**.

Draw straight lines between each number and letter to finish this touchscreen grid.

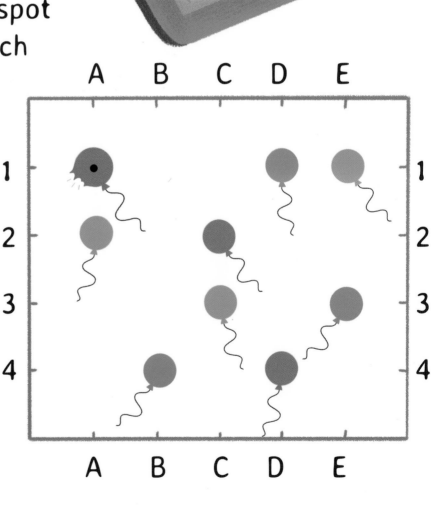

Find and **make a dot** at these places (intersections) on your grid to pop six balloons.

A̶1̶ C2 B4 E3 D1 A2

Well done!

The Internet

The **Internet** connects **computers** together so they can talk and share information around the world.

When you visit a **website**, what you see has been loaded over the Internet from another computer.

Can you find a **path** from one **computer** to the other? Watch out for the ones that aren't working!

Data travels through lots of other computers on its way to you. Can you find a different route back again?

START

The **World Wide Web** connects together **information** on computers on the Internet.

WEB PAGES

Typing a web address into a **web browser** allows you to ask for a **web page** from another computer. You can then click on **links** to access more information.

ICON
a visual symbol representing a subject

Where on these **web pages** would you **click** to find out about the weather?

What else do you think you could find out about from these web pages?

The World Wide Web was invented by Sir Tim Berners-Lee in 1989.

Well done!

How do computers communicate?

A lot of computers have a **Wi-Fi** chip that allows them to connect to the Internet **without wires**.

WI-FI SYMBOL

p	r	i	n	t	e	r
b	i	c	y	d	a	e
v	l	a	p	t	o	p
q	r	m	o	a	p	h
c	o	e	b	b	w	o
z	b	r	o	k	i	n
w	o	a	t	e	f	e
p	t	a	b	l	e	t

All these things can **connect** to Wi-Fi. Try to find them in the wordsearch.

phone   laptop   tablet

printer   camera   robot

Many computers also have a **Bluetooth** chip. Bluetooth is good for sharing data over small distances.

Bluetooth was named after a Scandinavian king who was known for unifying tribes.

Can you **draw** the Bluetooth logo without taking your pen off the page?

How are computers connected?

Wi-Fi is convenient, but not as fast as **physical cables**.

There are lots of cables **connecting** computers underground, between overhead poles and even under the sea.

YOU'VE GOT MAIL!

A friend sends a **message** from America. Follow the path the message takes with your pen.

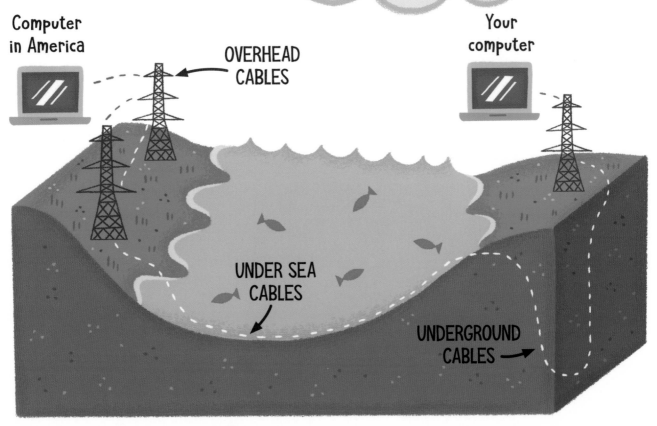

Computer in America

OVERHEAD CABLES

Your computer

UNDER SEA CABLES

UNDERGROUND CABLES

It used to take **weeks** to send a message by boat, now we can do it in **seconds!**

Well done!

What is the Cloud?

Cloud computing allows you to **store** information and data on other computers (the Cloud).

You can then **access the Cloud** using applications, and get to your data from any computer.

Draw a line to match the **app** or **program** to the data in the cloud.

photo viewer

music app

word processor

video player

email app

Why can't my tablet go faster?

Does your tablet sometimes seem **slow**? Why can't it go faster?

Tick all the **correct** reasons.

☐ 1. The **processor** can't process instructions fast enough to keep up with the apps that are running.

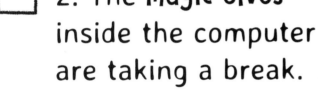

☐ 2. The **magic elves** inside the computer are taking a break.

☐ 3. The computer is loading data from **storage**, which is slower than memory.

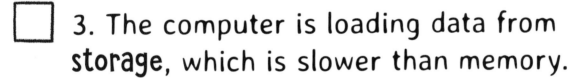

☐ 4. The computer is loading data from **the Internet** or waiting for a reply from another computer.

Well done!

ANSWERS: The most likely reasons are 1, 3 and 4

Past and future of computers

One of the **first computers** was designed by **Tommy Flowers** at Bletchley Park, England in 1943.

This computer helped decode messages during World War II.

Starting at C, follow the **arrows** then write down the letters to find out what the first computer was called.

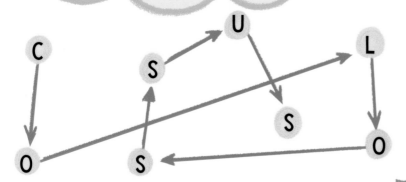

C _____

means big and important. This computer filled a **whole room!**

As computers are getting **smaller** and **faster, inventors** can put computers into more and more gadgets.

Draw a picture of a **gadget** you'd like to invent.